D0874336

Alexander Graham Bell

The Man Behind the Telephone

by Sally Lee

PEBBLE
a capstone imprint

Little Explorer is published by Pebble,
1710 Roe Crest Drive, North Mankato, Minnesota 56003
www.capstonepub.com

The name of the Smithsonian Institution and the sunburst
logo are registered trademarks of the Smithsonian Institution.
For more information, please visit www.si.edu.

Library of Congress Cataloging-in-Publication Data is available on the Library of Congress website.
ISBN 978-1-9771-0975-0 (library binding)
ISBN 978-1-9771-1055-8 (paperback)
ISBN 978-1-9771-0985-9 (eBook PDF)

Summary: A world without telephones? Impossible for most young readers to imagine. Let them know
they can thank inventor Alexander Graham Bell for every ringtone! Filled with facts and photos, Bell's
story highlights the scientific process he followed, failures and all, from identifying a problem to getting
his communication technology into the hands of users.

Editorial Credits
Jill Kalz, editor; Kayla Rossow, designer; Svetlana Zhurkin, media researcher;
Tori Abraham, production specialist

Our very special thanks to Emma Grahn, Spark!Lab Manager, Lemelson Center for the Study of
Invention and Innovation, National Museum of American History. Capstone would also like to thank
Kealy Gordon, Product Development Manager, and the following at Smithsonian Enterprises: Ellen
Nanney, Licensing Manager; Brigid Ferraro, Vice President, Education and Consumer Products; and
Carol LeBlanc, Senior Vice President, Education and Consumer Products.

Image Credits
Alamy: The Picture Art Collection, 18; Library of Congress, cover (right), 5, 6, 8, 12, 13, 20, 21 (bottom),
23, 27, 29, Carol M. Highsmith Archive, 19; Mary Evans Picture Library: Grenville Collins Postcard
Collection, 14; National Archives and Records Administration, 22; Newscom: akg-images, 10, World
History Archive, 25; North Wind Picture Archives, 7; Science Source: SPL, 11; Shutterstock: Adrio
Communications Ltd, cover (left), Chris Hellyar, 17, Everett Historical, 15, 16, 21 (top), 26, 28, Monkey
Business Images, 4, Vladimir Satylganov, 9 (bottom); Smithsonian Institution: National Museum of
American History, 24; SuperStock: Pantheon, 9 (top)

Design Elements by Shutterstock

All internet sites appearing in back matter were available and accurate when this book was sent to press.

Printed in the United States of America.
PA70

TABLE OF CONTENTS

INTRODUCTION

Imagine not having a phone. Tough, isn't it? Telephones are a part of our daily lives, like cars, computers, and fast food. But there was a time when phones didn't exist.

Then, in the mid-1800s, a man named Alexander Graham Bell was born. His curious nature pushed him to explore many kinds of ideas, especially those about sound. And the world would be forever changed by his greatest invention—the telephone.

Telephones connect us to one another.

Alexander chose his own middle name when he was 10 years old. His father had a friend named Graham.

Alexander had two brothers. Melville (Melly) was older, and Edward (Ted) was younger.

Alexander (middle) learned much from his grandpa (left) and father (right).

Alexander Graham Bell was born in Scotland in 1847. He was a smart, curious boy who loved solving problems. These traits helped him become a good inventor. He made his first invention at age 12, for a local flour mill. The invention removed husks from grains of wheat.

Young Alexander enjoyed discovering new things.

Alexander's mother taught him at home until he was 10 years old. He then went to Royal High School, finishing at age 14 with average grades.

Alexander had a
special way of talking
to his mother. He put
his lips on her
forehead and spoke in
a low voice.

Alexander's mother was nearly deaf. His father helped people with hearing and speech problems. These facts made Alexander want to spend his life helping others who could not hear.

In the 1800s some people who were deaf used devices such as this to try to learn how to speak.

Alexander's mother
loved to play the
piano. She put an ear
trumpet on the piano
to hear the music.

7

When Alexander was 14 years old, he spent a year in London, England, with his grandfather. Like Alexander's father, Grandpa Bell also helped people learn to speak better. He made his grandson study hard and always dress well.

When he was just 16 years old, Alexander began teaching speech and piano at a private school. He was younger than some of his students!

Alexander Bell inspired his grandson to do great things.

Alexander's interest in sound grew after a year in London in 1862.

Alexander watched his grandfather give speech lessons. He read books about the human voice. His year in London changed him from a boy to a man.

Alexander knew that piano strings had to vibrate to make music. Knowing this fact helped him with some of his inventions later in life.

9

THE TALKING HEAD

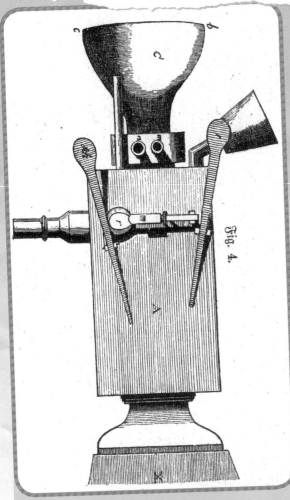

One of the earliest speaking machines was Wolfgang von Kempelen's, created in the late 1700s.

After he returned from London, Bell and his father saw a "speaking machine." The box made voice-like sounds. Bell's father dared him and his brother Melly to make a better one.

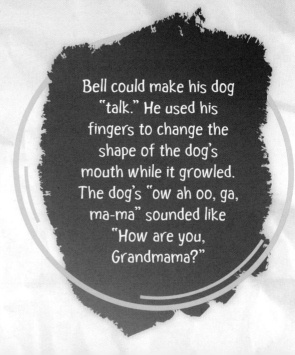

Bell could make his dog "talk." He used his fingers to change the shape of the dog's mouth while it growled. The dog's "ow ah oo, ga, ma-ma" sounded like "How are you, Grandmama?"

Alexander and Melly learned how the mouth and throat made sounds by reading their father's books.

Joseph Faber created a speaking machine with a woman's face in the mid-1800s.

The brothers built a talking head. Bell made the mouth parts. Melly made a tube for the throat. While Melly blew through the tube, Bell moved the mouth. Their head cried, "Mamma, Mamma." The neighbors thought a baby was crying!

PICTURING SPEECH

Bell's father invented a way for people who were deaf to *see* voice sounds. He called it Visible Speech. He drew symbols for every sound the human voice could make. The symbols showed how the throat, tongue, and lips needed to be placed to make each sound.

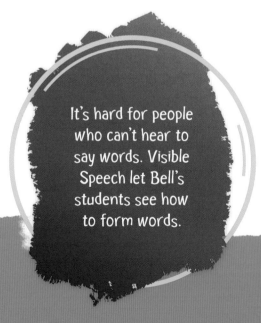

It's hard for people who can't hear to say words. Visible Speech let Bell's students see how to form words.

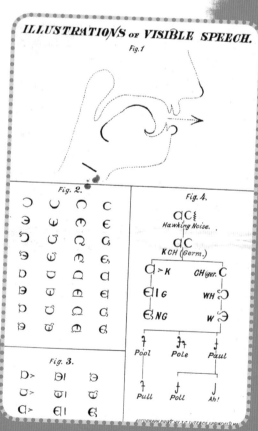

Bell's father made Visible Speech work with any language, not just English.

Bell helped his father show people how Visible Speech worked. After Bell left a room, people suggested sounds to his father. His father then wrote down the symbols for each sound. When Bell came back, he looked at the symbols and repeated every sound just right.

Bell once visited a Mohawk village in Canada. He used Visible Speech to record many of their words. In exchange the American Indians taught Bell their war dance.

BIG CHANGES

Today the Bell house in Brantford, Ontario, is a Canadian National Historic Site because of the telephone-related work Bell did there.

By 1870 both of Bell's brothers had died. Bell and his parents moved to Canada. There Bell set up a home lab. He did experiments with sounds and electricity.

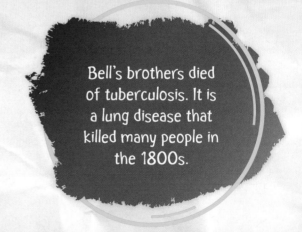

Bell's brothers died of tuberculosis. It is a lung disease that killed many people in the 1800s.

Bell found a book by a German scientist. Unfortunately Bell couldn't read German well. He thought the scientist had sent all speech sounds over a wire. In truth it was only vowel sounds. But Bell believed all speech could be turned into electrical signals. The belief made him keep trying.

Most of Bell's early inventions came from his desire to help his students. Bell's goal was to help people who were deaf live better in the hearing world.

Bell's interest in sending sounds began with the telegraph. Samuel Morse invented it in 1837. The telegraph sent messages over wires. It used a code made up of long and short bursts of electricity. The bursts went to a receiver that changed them into dots and dashes on a paper tape. A person then decoded the marks.

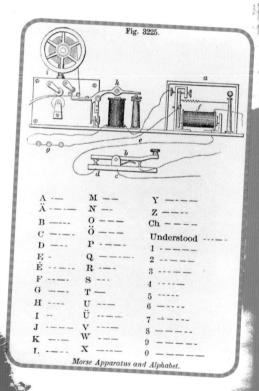

Morse Apparatus and Alphabet.

Bell had an early interest in the telegraph. He once made his own. He strung a wire from his room to a friend's house.

Long, thick piano strings have the lowest pitch.

Music gave Bell an idea. He thought several messages could be sent along the same telegraph wire. But each message would have to be at a different pitch.

Bell saw a problem. Only one message could be sent at a time. He wanted to find a way to send several telegraph messages at once.

Bell learned about pitch from playing the piano. Pitch is how high or low a sound is. Things that vibrate fast have a higher pitch.

MOVING TO BOSTON

In 1871, at age 24, Bell moved to Boston, Massachusetts, to teach people who were deaf. He taught classes and also worked with private students. One was Mabel Hubbard. She had gotten scarlet fever as a child. It had left her unable to hear.

Bell used an alphabet glove with his students. They could spell words by pointing to letters on the glove.

Bell (top, far right) taught at the Boston School for the Deaf.

Mabel's father liked Bell's ideas. He and another student's father gave Bell money to work on the new telegraph. Bell taught during the day and worked on his invention at night.

Bell's Boston laboratory was in the attic of a downtown building.

Bell used a musical term for his invention. He called it the harmonic telegraph.

Bell's ear phonautograph was a machine that turned sound vibrations into visible waves. Bell thought his students could learn to speak if they matched the waves they made to those of people who could hear.

LUCKY ACCIDENT

Bell had good ideas. But he needed help to make them work. He hired a man named Thomas Watson. Watson knew a lot about machines and electricity. First Bell drew sketches of his ideas. Then Watson used the drawings to build models.

Thomas Watson helped create the telephone.

Many of Bell's ideas failed. Still he refused to give up. He believed that every experiment taught him a helpful lesson.

Bell wanted to work on his telephone idea. Hubbard's father wanted him to keep working on the telegraph. Bell stayed up late many nights to work on both.

One night a part on Watson's receiver stuck. He plucked it with his finger. Bell heard a "ping" through his transmitter. The sound had traveled along the wires! Bell had proof. Now he was sure that voices could be sent along wires too.

Mabel Hubbard's parents

Bell fell in love with Mabel Hubbard. At first her parents thought he was not a good match for their daughter. Bell worked hard to prove them wrong.

Success came on March 10, 1876. Bell and Watson were in different rooms. "Mr. Watson, come here. I want you!" Bell said into his mouthpiece. Watson rushed into the room. He had heard every word!

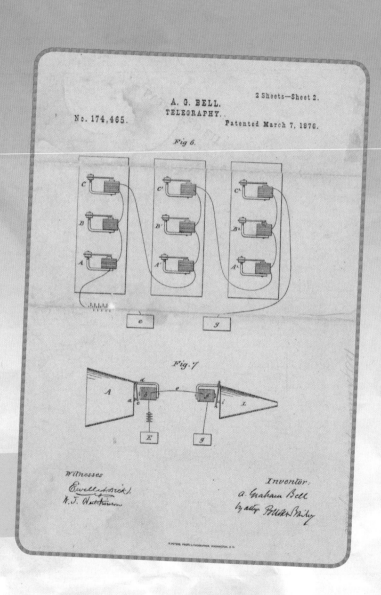

Bell made these drawings to show how his telephone worked.

A few months later, Bell showed his telephone at a world's fair. He won the prize for the best electrical machine.

Bell and his investors formed the Bell Telephone Company on July 9, 1877.

Bell's family, including his wife, Mabel, and daughters Elsie (left) and Marian, around 1885

Bell married Mabel Hubbard on July 11, 1877. They went to England to show more people the telephone.

Bell's telephone was a success. But there was a problem. Other inventors had been working on telephone-like devices at the same time as Bell. Some men said their inventions had come first.

Whoever was first would have special rights. No one else would be allowed to make or sell that invention. Bell spent years fighting legal battles to prove his device was first. In the end, he won.

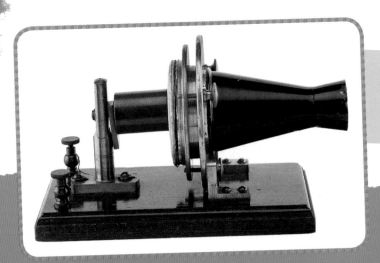

Bell's 1876 model was made of wood, brass, and tin.

In 1879 Bell moved to Washington, D.C. The next year he won a prize from the French government for inventing the telephone. He used the prize money to open the Volta Laboratory. There he and his partners did experiments with sound.

THE GREATEST INVENTION

Bell thought the photophone was his greatest invention. It was able to send sounds over a beam of light instead of through wires. Although it didn't catch on, it led to today's fiber optics. Bell even wanted to name one baby daughter "Photophone." Mabel wouldn't let him.

NEW IDEAS

Bell invented things to solve other problems too. In 1881 U.S. President James Garfield was shot. Bell made a metal detector to try to find the bullet left in the president's body. The metal springs on Garfield's bed kept the detector from working right.

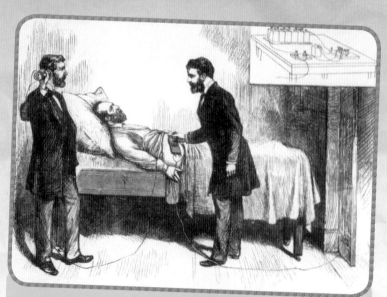

Bell's detector sent a buzzing sound through an earphone when it found metal.

Bell did not invent things all by himself. He put together groups of talented people to help him.

Two of Bell's sons died soon after birth. They were born too early and couldn't breathe on their own. Bell invented the "vacuum jacket." It forced air into and out of the lungs. It led to the invention of the iron lung.

Bell also improved the inventions of others. One was Thomas Edison's phonograph. Bell invented round, flat records. They made it easier to record and play back sounds.

UP IN THE AIR

In the early 1890s, Bell moved his family to Nova Scotia, Canada. There he experimented with flight. He started by building kites. Then he used what he learned from testing the kites to design and build airplanes. Bell and four other men formed a company. Their airplane, the Silver Dart, was the first plane to fly in Canada, in 1909.

Alexander Graham Bell died in 1922. He was 75 years old. Bell's invention of the telephone changed the way people talked to each other. Today it is used all over the world. But Bell never thought the telephone was his most important success. He was most proud of his work helping people who could not hear.

Bell filled pages with handwritten notes and drawings.

Bell refused to have a telephone in his study. He thought it would distract him from his work.

to one side before the stop
the Capsule seems to promise to be a real delicate galvanometer
for the Undulatory current.   Still simpler forms
may be made. I like that shown   page 13 (Fig 3)
if the cylindrical iron core can be fitted tightly but
this would impede its motion.

Thoughts.

Improved forms of the "Flame-Galvanometer".

Compare Fig 3 with that
on page 13. Both ends
of the coil (C) are plugged
up. One end A with iron.
The other end B with a piece
of wood containing two pipes communicating respectively with D the
gas-pipe and E the burner. The loose-fitting iron-
cylinder F is free to vibrate against A.   Fig 4
Would not an iron gas-pipe A (Fig 4)
placed within a helix (H) through which
discontinuous (or undulatory?) current
is passing be thrown into molecular
vibration — and hence cause
vibrations in the glass and in the flame F.

De la Rive states that flames change their shape
when brought near the poles of an electro-magnet.
If this is so a vibratory current of electricity should impart a
vibratory motion to the flame placed near the
poles of an electro-magnet on circuit.

Fig 5 shows one form
of Flame-Galvanometer for the
Undulatory current —   The
flame F is merely placed between
the poles S, N of an electro-magnet
on circuit.

Figs 6 and 7 show new experimental Transmitter con-
sisting of a Sounding-board upon which is the coil (C). A
permanent magnet NS is supported in a block of india-rubber
so that a sound made near the sounding board
so that the coil I will vibrate with it
of the magnet NS will occasion undulations
Noted February 23d 1876
by A. Graham Bell

GLOSSARY

detector—a device that finds something

ear trumpet—a horn-shaped tube once used as a hearing aid by those with poor hearing

fiber optics—a way of sending information through thin threads of glass or plastic in the form of light signals

harmonic—using musical notes played at the same time to make a pleasing sound

husk—the dry outer covering of some seeds and fruits

inventor—a person who thinks up and makes something new

investor—someone who puts money into a business and shares in its earning

iron lung—a large machine once used to help people breathe when they couldn't do it on their own

Mohawk—a member of an American Indian people who live in northern New York and Canada

phonograph—a record player

photophone—a kind of telephone that sent sounds over beams of light, rather than wires

pitch—the highness or lowness of a sound

receiver—a device that collects electronic signals and changes them into something that can be seen, heard, or understood

symbol—something that stands for something else

transmitter—a device that sends sounds or signals

vibrate—to move back and forth very rapidly and steadily

visible—able to be seen

CRITICAL THINKING QUESTIONS

1. Why was Alexander Graham Bell so interested in sounds throughout his life?

2. From whom did Bell receive help with his many inventions? Name at least two people and describe how they helped.

3. How has the telephone changed since Bell first invented it?

READ MORE

Fraser, Mary Ann. *Alexander Graham Bell Answers the Call.* Watertown, MA: Charlesbridge, 2017.

Kramer, Barbara. *Alexander Graham Bell.* National Geographic Kids. Washington, DC: National Geographic, 2015.

Spengler, Kremena T. *An Illustrated Timeline of Inventions and Inventors.* Visual Timelines in History. Mankato, MN: Picture Window Books, 2012.

INTERNET SITES

Animated video of first telephone call
https://www.youtube.com/watch?v=yNA6kiL2IRo

Animated video of planning the telephone
https://www.youtube.com/watch?v=2BCvXH5M9n0

How to make a can-and-string telephone, with information about sound
https://www.youtube.com/watch?v=3yqB2KFwJCo

INDEX